A Story Is to Share

How Ruth Krauss
Found Another Way
to Tell a Tale

words by CARTER HIGGINS

pictures by ISABELLE ARSENAULT

Abrams Books for Young Readers • New York

Born
a baby
late at night

There's
no parade

just crashing

rain

Soon
the girl
twirls upside-up
and rides her bike
down down the hall

But sickness sticks around a lot
and steals her voice away—

so she wiggle-wiggles little fingers
that's how she says hi

Like this

She listens listens
writes and draws

stitches pages
sews a book

She finds another way
to tell a tale

Then
this girl
grows up a bit
picks up a violin

Like this

But the right way
is the wrong way
and the near way
is too far away
it hurts
her neck
to hold it still
and music is to play

She has to squeak a new sound

with a *tweedle-eedle-oodle*

A wall can make a *bum-boom-boom*

the floor a *fa-la-lunk*

She finds another way
to play a song

Then
this girl
at summer camp
way deep deep
in the woods

likes backward clothes
and fortunes told
she's ready for a show

She dances when she shouldn't
wears a shoelace for a tie

Like this

She cheers for friends
who make up rules
and share a midnight feast

She finds another way
to be herself

All grown up now
and a painter
in a town
always awake

She works from late
till light
for days
stirs many
glugs and globs
of pink
to find a shade as sweet
as this
a dainty dusty
rose

It's good to paint and whoosh and whirl

to waint and whoosh and pearl

Like this

She finds another way
to ploosh and swirl

She sees stories
in wiggles
and music
and costumes
and painting

So what about
words ?

Now
a writer
with ideas
and thoughts
just right for books

Like this

but people say

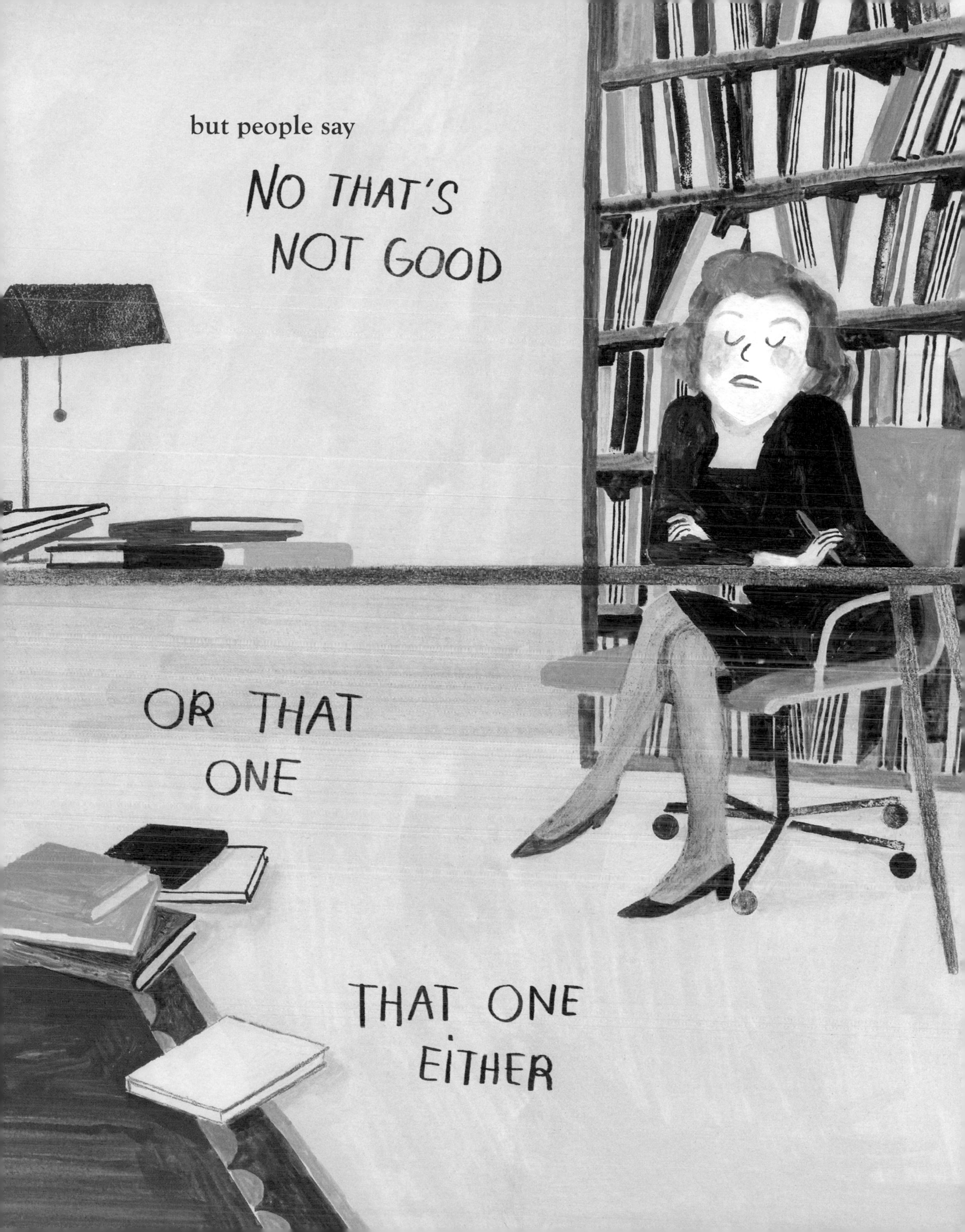

So she covers all the tables
with some crayons
papers
pens

and she scribbles when she wants to
and she doodles

and she scratches

Or she crumples up the paper
sticks a pin into the ink
and she scrambles up the sounds

Like this

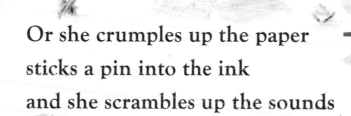

she thinks and plays and plans
until—

What happens when ideas get stuck
or when the stories hush?

What happens when you
chase
them
and
they scatter?

Here's
her neighbor
much much smaller
he sees the world
he says the words

Like her

His hand holds some seeds
and they plant them
in dirt
and they wait for the carrot to grow

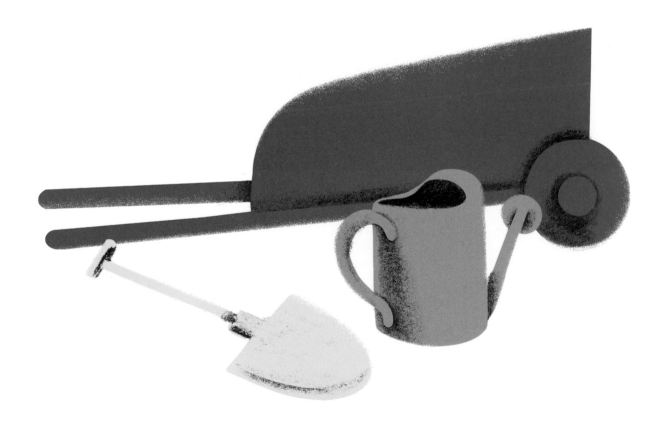

When she listens
and she wonders

and she's playful
she remembers

She finds another way
to tell a tale

Author's Note

In her book *Open House for Butterflies*, she wrote, "There should be a parade when a baby is born." But in Baltimore, in the middle of the night, in July of 1901, there was only a storm when Ruth Ida Krauss arrived in this world.

And so was she—a whirlwind of wit and words, sensitive and inquisitive. She wanted to be an acrobat and spent much of her childhood walking around on her hands. But Ruth was often sick, battling earaches and appendicitis and whooping cough and chicken pox. So she rode her bike inside the house when she was too ill to go outside.

Stories brought her comfort. She read them, listened to them, and made her own books. As a teenager, she wrote them in a secret language and hid those special books from her parents.

Ruth began to tell stories in other ways too, like through the strings of her violin. Instead of holding it correctly, she'd press one end to a wall or a wooden door or bathroom tile to create unusual sounds, a twist on the expected. At Camp Walden, she wore her clothes backwards, her friends called her Doggie, and she preferred dancing to athletic contests. She had an itch to paint, to swirl color around, to become an artist. So she did that too, graduating from Parsons School of Design in New York.

She was married once before finding her great love, Crockett Johnson, known to Ruth and his friends as Dave. While Dave worked as a cartoonist, Ruth studied anthropology, language, progressive ideas, and social prejudices. She wanted to fit those big ideas into a small book. Ruth's editor would ultimately be the legendary Ursula Nordstrom, who agreed to meet Ruth at the urging of her assistant, Charlotte Zolotow. The two were smitten with Ruth from the start and hoped she would write a book for them.

Ruth loved children and hated injustice, so she wrote for both. None of her ideas were quite right at first. But soon, an imagined conversation with her five-year-old neighbor became *The Carrot Seed*, one hundred or so words of hope and grit and *kid-ness*.

Ruth had found her story. Dave illustrated it.

That seed sprouted many more stories that grew from Ruth's grand kinship to children. She connected with the Bank Street Writers Laboratory, which became just that for Ruth: a place to explore kids' thinking, their language, their nonsense, their ferocious feelings, a place that echoed Ruth's respect for children as real, true people—fully-formed humans rather than miniature, *less-than* grown-ups.

This is what makes Ruth's books special: the way she watched the world with her eyes and heart wide open. The way she honored children and their curiosity. The way she asked one, "What is a hole for?" and received a heartfelt answer that became a literary sensation.

That book, *A Hole Is to Dig*, was also the debut of legendary illustrator Maurice Sendak.

Other potential collaborators called Ruth's text "fragmentary" and "elusive," but when Ruth saw Maurice's sketchbook, she knew his small people were a perfect match for her fantastic and effervescent words.

And they were.

The two worked on *A Hole Is to Dig* at Ruth and Dave's quiet home in the integrated neighborhood of Rowayton, in Norwalk, Connecticut. It was the 1950s, and this trio was as good a family as any other.

Always aware of injustice, some of Ruth's final requests for changes to Maurice's art were to ensure that boys and girls both were represented without regard to gendered stereotypes. Childhood doesn't care whether you are a boy or a girl, and neither would the pages of their masterpiece.

Ruth and Dave collaborated on a new book during this time as well, *How to Make an Earthquake*. Ruth was again in and out of sickness, and Dave provided steady bowls of chocolate ice cream and quiet time to dream. While he took care of her, he dreamed up a hero of his own, a small boy with a purple crayon. His name was Harold.

Ruth lost Dave to cancer in 1975, and she lived without him for another eighteen years. During that time, she continued to tell stories in many different ways, from writer to poet to playwright and back to writer, and in 1987, her last children's book, *Big and Little*, was published. Ruth was disappointed and angry that the book's illustrator only painted white children, and she never wrote another book again.

Ruth and Dave never had children of their own, but they kept all the children of their imaginations tucked under their wings—the mischief-makers, the carrot growers, and the ones that *hooie hooie hooie*. In the months preceding her death, Ruth took in a young family with a small child as boarders. That small child, Bianca, was three and a half years old when Ruth died in 1993, and she was the last to leave her side.

A raging storm brought her into the world, and a child gently showed her out. Ruth Krauss wrote the time in between.

On a piece of paper

I write it.

—*Ruth Krauss, I Write It*

Select Bibliography

"Krauss, Ruth." *American National Biography Online*. September 2005.

Nel, Philip. *Crockett Johnson and Ruth Krauss: How an Unlikely Couple Found Love, Dodged the FBI, and Transformed Children's Literature*. Jackson, MS: University of Mississippi, 2012.

——. "It's a Wild World: Maurice Sendak, Wild Things, and Childhood." *Nine Kinds of Pie* (blog). October 13, 2013. See philnel.com/2013/10/15/wildthings.

——. "A Very Special House." *Nine Kinds of Pie* (blog). September 30, 2014. See philnel.com/2014/09/30/veryspecialhouse.

"Ruth Krauss, 91, Dies; A Writer for Children." *New York Times*. July 14, 1993.

Ruth Krauss Papers. Archives & Special Collections at the Thomas J. Dodd Research Center. University of Connecticut Library.

Featured Books Written by Ruth Krauss

The Carrot Seed, illustrated by Crockett Johnson, New York: Harper, 1945.

A Hole Is to Dig: A First Book of First Definitions, illustrated by Maurice Sendak, New York: Harper, 1952.

A Very Special House, illustrated by Maurice Sendak, New York: Harper, 1953.

How to Make an Earthquake, illustrated by Crockett Johnson, New York: Harper, 1954.

Open House for Butterflies, illustrated by Maurice Sendak, New York: Harper, 1960.

I Write It, illustrated by Mary Chalmers, New York: Harper and Row, 1970.

Big and Little, illustrated by Mary Szilagyi, New York: Scholastic, 1987.

For Rubin Pfeffer —C.H.

To Florent and his Florent's way of doing things —I.A.

The illustrations for this book were created with ink, watercolor, and gouache, with digital touchups.

Cataloging-in-Publication Data has been applied for and may be obtained from the Library of Congress.

ISBN 978-1-4197-4993-3

Text copyright © 2022 Carter Higgins
Illustrations copyright © 2022 Isabelle Arsenault
Book design by Pamela Notarantonio

Printed and bound in China
10 9 8 7 6 5 4 3 2 1

Abrams Books for Young Readers are available at special discounts when purchased in quantity for premiums and promotions as well as fundraising or educational use. Special editions can also be created to specification. For details, contact specialsales@abramsbooks.com or the address below.

Abrams® is a registered trademark of Harry N. Abrams, Inc.

ABRAMS The Art of Books
195 Broadway, New York, NY 10007
abramsbooks.com